A Summary of Robert C. Pozen's Book:

Extreme Productivity

Boost Your Results, Reduce Your Hours

by Shortcut Summaries

Published by CornerTrade Publishing,
a subsidiary of CornerTrade, LLC

ISBN: 1481241931
ISBN-13: 978-1481241939

Extreme Productivity

Copyright © 2012 CornerTrade, LLC

Disclaimer

Contents

Contents Continued

PREFACE

Summary of Robert Pozen's *Extreme Productivity*

In Extreme Productivity, Bob Pozen, senior fellow at the Brookings Institution and a senior lecturer at the prestigious Harvard Business School, gives real-world, easy-to-follow guidelines for increasing professional and personal productivity. These guidelines are based on Pozen's own experiences in the corporate world.

Section One shows you how to organize your priorities through a simple set of to-do lists. Next comes Section Two, with suggestions on how to streamline your everyday routine.

Section Three offers personal skills that are highly

beneficial to productivity, while Section Four tackles the tough job of managing both your employees and your supervisor.

In Section Five, Pozen offers suggestions on creating and maintaining a high level of productivity throughout your entire lifetime, including the all-important aspects of balancing your home and professional lives.

While written mainly for the current or aspiring professional, Pozen's book is applicable to virtually anybody at any stage in life, from the high school student to the retiree. These are not magic bullets, rather concrete methods intended to become lifelong habits.

Increased productivity allows us to lead more balanced, efficient and relaxed lives, which translates into a better quality of life at any stage.

Extreme Productivity Section 1

Focus and Prioritizing

In becoming more productive, your very first step is creating simple yet organized to-do lists. These can be either written out by hand or created electronically; use the method easiest for you. Pozen offers six simple steps for creating your list(s).

Write it all down – Every single work-related task, objective or goal you have needs to be identified. You will organize them later; for now, just get them written down.

Time Organization – Separate your list into three smaller lists based on time goals. These should include lifetime professional goals, yearly goals and weekly tasks and activities.

Ranking Yearly Goals – This step is divided into three sub-steps. Consider these things: What you enjoy doing, what your strengths are and what is expected of you. Things that your employees or boss expects of you must come before things you simply want to do, although including your wants is important as well.

Ranking Weekly Tasks – Tasks, for most people, are either jobs assigned to them or steps that move them closer to a lifetime or yearly goal. Separate your tasks into these categories.

Determine Time Usage – Most people waste more time then they realize. In order to figure out where you have room to improve, take a look at your calendar or your digital day planner. Examining your current work schedule, determine how much time you actually spend at work or working, the three things you spend the most time doing while at work, and how much time you spend weekly in meetings, doing paperwork or answering e-mails.

Next, look at your future work schedule. Do you anticipate any changes, or do you expect your schedule and activities to look pretty much the same? Do you anticipate or want progress? In which ways and areas? What will this progress look like, and what, conversely, would failure in this area look like?

To complete this step, examine how you spend your

time now compared with your goals. Are you devoting time to truly important things, or wasting hours with busywork?

Address and Fix Imbalances – Focus on any areas that could use improvement. If you're spending hours a day replying to e-mails that don't further any of your goals, this is an imbalance. How you fix these imbalances will depend heavily on your position within your company. A CEO can shift things around fairly easily; a lower-level employee usually can't.

If you're not in a position to create changes, it's time for some creative thinking regarding how to work around and with established rules. For example, you may have some tasks you can easily delegate to an employee. Condense and eliminate as many unnecessary or low-level tasks as you can, and use the extra time for something that furthers your goals.

Focusing on Priorities First

Spending too much time on unnecessary tasks is one of the biggest time-wasters out there. Pozen suggests that once priorities have been identified, they should take up the largest portion of your time.

There are many ways to approach a big project, many of which waste time. Focusing on the end result instead of getting caught up in the little details allows you to be more productive. Identify the critical issues upon which the success of the project rests, and brainstorm how best to resolve these issues. This end-result-first approach allows you to pare down your concentration to items and tasks that further the project, instead of wasting time on details that can be delegated, are not crucial to the outcome, or may simply fall to the wayside once larger issues are tackled.

Checking Each Project in Progress

Once you are approximately halfway through a project, Pozen recommends taking fresh stock of the situation. You may find that priorities have stayed the same, but you might also discover new ways to save time. Certain aspects you once thought were vital may not be as important as they were before. Refresh your lists and delegations accordingly.

Procrastination – The Efficiency Drain

We're all guilty of procrastinating occasionally. The sooner and more completely you can cut this time-waster out of your life, the closer you'll come to ultimate productivity. Different types of procrastinators respond to varying types of motivation.

If you waste time because a project seems too intimidatingly large, break it down into smaller pieces. If distractions like Facebook or television are diverting your attention, be ruthless in removing them from your workspace so they don't have a chance to catch your eye. Some chronic procrastinators actually harbor a deep-seated belief that regardless of how hard they try, it won't be good enough. Pozen suggests that if you think you have this fear, professional help may necessary to work through your procrastination issues.

Rewards and accountability are often helpful for moderate to mild procrastinators. You might give yourself a small reward – a snack or some leisure time – for completing a certain task. Accountability is built into some projects, but if you're working without a deadline and this leads you to procrastinate, create your own deadlines and then hand them over to somebody else. This second-party accountability helps you keep yourself on track, even if there are no "official" deadlines on your schedule.

Quality Versus Quantity

Simply because you're at your desk (or in any work environment) doesn't mean you're getting things accomplished. You may still be getting paid, but you can easily be surfing the internet or staring out the window. Instead of focusing on the hours you spend at work, Pozen suggests focusing on the work you actually get done.

For employees, this can be quite difficult. You don't

create your schedule, so you need to be at work regardless of whether you're working or not. In this case, creative thinking is important. See how you can shift things around within the boundaries of your position. For example, if you typically don't receive your daily assignments until the afternoon, you may be able to use your morning hours doing something more productive than standing around and chatting with your colleagues. Be creative with your time; just don't do anything that could jeopardize your job. Hourly employees will have the hardest time with this objective. If you work for an hourly wage, look for ways to "sneak" productivity into your downtime.

Letting Small Tasks Go

Many of us are guilty of obsessing over – or at least devoting too much time to – small, rather irrelevant tasks. Pozen suggests an easy way to manage these tasks. Handle each one immediately by deciding whether to discard or respond to it. Emails are a wonderful illustration. Pozen's recommendation is that approximately 80% of all your emails can be legitimately ignored. The remaining 20% should be handled right away so your can focus on other activities. Resisting the urge to go back and "check" on things you've already handled is a huge time-saver, and it allows you to put all your attention right where it needs to be – on the task at hand.

Handling small tasks usually falls into one of two

categories. Very small items can (and usually should) be completed immediately so they are out of your mind. If something needs slightly more work, such as an email that requires some research, place it on your to-do list, with a specified time for completion. Filing away these small tasks ensures that you'll not only get them done on time, but that your attention won't be taken up with them unnecessarily while working on other, more important tasks.

Streamlining the time you spend on emails can be accomplished rather simply. Pozen suggests setting a time to check and respond (or file) emails, rather than impulsively checking in all day long. Avoid sending unnecessary emails yourself – there's usually no need for a one-word reply, so don't waste the time.

How and When to Multitask

Pozen asserts that while multitasking is a wonderful way to increase productivity, it has its time and place. It is best for managing several small-scale tasks at once, such as eating your lunch while reviewing your email. Items that require your full and undivided attention should not be combined.

Pozen also cautions against multitasking in front of customers, while meeting with your superiors, or while performing any task on which you need to appear completely focused, such as giving a presentation. Be sure to limit your multitasking to issues that can legitimately be managed with only part of your brain.

Losing Perfectionist Habits

Demanding perfection in every task is a waste. Not every email needs to be worded perfectly, for example. Kicking your perfectionist habits allows you to focus only on those issues that actually benefit from extreme attention to detail.

Navigating Frustrating Rules

Rules are generally created with good intentions, but over time they can lead to wasted time due to unnecessary steps.

Researching the actual purpose of seemingly pointless rules can provide some insight. If there is a legitimate reason your superiors want something done a certain way, you're unlikely to change their minds. Learn about the rule, work with it and figure out a way to do so without getting annoyed.

Key Points of Extreme Productivity Section 1

Prioritizing goals and then focusing the most energy on your highest priorities is crucial to productivity.

All of your tasks should be written down, organized and ranked according to importance.

Rank and organize according to what you enjoy, what your strengths are, what others expect from you and what does (and doesn't) further your goals.

Comparing priorities to time usage is crucial, and will probably show you room for improvement. Determine the reason you're wasting time and delegate, organize or change your habits to improve productivity.

Time spent at work does not necessarily correlate to the quality of your work. Adopt this mindset and treat others accordingly.

Tackle projects beginning with the desired result. Halfway through projects, step back and re-assess to determine if any goals or tasks need altering.

Use any means necessary to stop procrastinating, whether that means a tasty reward, being accountable to another person or seeking professional help.

Give yourself permission to ignore low-priority tasks, and realize that approximately 80% of tasks fall into this category. If something does warrant your attention, complete the task right away or properly file it for later.

Do something well the first time and then let it be. Don't obsess.

Learn to multitask properly. Use it for low-level tasks. Avoid it with superiors, customers and in any situation that demands your full attention.

Streamline your email. Ask for co-workers' cooperation if necessary.

Learn to accept imperfect work on low-priority tasks in order to put perfectionism to good use on important ones.

Time-wasting rules can be dealt with by changing them or working around them. Determine what you're able to change and avoid wasting time being frustrated over things you can't.

Extreme Productivity Section 2

Productivity in Everyday Life

How you structure your day can have a huge effect, positively or negatively, on your productivity. In Section Two, Pozen shows how to streamline your everyday routine to increase productivity through simplification, organization and remaining alert.

Planning Your Day

Although there are many types of to-do lists you can use, Pozen offers his own as an example. Drawing a line down the middle of a piece of paper (or doing something similar electronically), place your tasks for the day on the left-hand side. Leave gaps in between each task. This is important for two reasons – time for free thought often results in great ideas, and it also avoids a disaster if a colleague is stuck in traffic, a meeting runs late or some other unforeseen occurrence disrupts your schedule.

On the right side of your list, write down notes about each task. For example, if have need to take part in a conference call at 10:30, what needs to be accomplished during that call? Not only does this keep you on track, but it might result in some extra time if you can resolve your conference-call issue early.

At the bottom of your daily list, leave space for things that you'd like to get done, but don't have a definite deadline. Add notes as you did for your must-do tasks, and rank these "should-do" items in order of priority.

Ensure that your list is portable. Keep it with you (or accessible) at all times, and adjust and make new notes as necessary.

Routines Fuel Productivity

It's easy to get distracted and delayed by hectic mornings. Pozen suggests streamlining your mornings as much as possible for a quick and hassle-free start to the day. Some studies suggest that even the simplest choices – berries or bananas on your oatmeal? - can tire the brain. Keep things simple to retain as much brain power as possible for more important decisions. Pozen suggests a narrow field of breakfast choices as well as choosing and laying out your clothing the night before.

Your time spent at the gym and running errands should be similarly scheduled ahead of time in order to minimize last-minute decisions and delays.

Lunch should be very simple as well. Unless you need to eat at a restaurant with a client, Pozen suggests a simple sandwich at your desk. Not only does this allow you to multitask while you eat, but it cuts down on time and choices.

Napping for Productivity

While it may sound counter-productive at first, Pozen asserts that taking a nap during the day actually helps improve focus and, therefore, productivity. If you have trouble falling asleep at work, find a quiet space and use a sleep mask over your eyes. Set your cell phone or other alarm to go off in thirty minutes, giving yourself plenty of time to refresh and renew your brain power. Taking your nap shortly after you've eaten lunch is considered best, since many of us tend to feel tired at this time and trying to slog through important projects with a foggy mind only leads to mistakes and wasted time.

Commuting and Family Time

Try to make it a routine to leave work in time to spend quality time with your family. Not only is this highly beneficial for children, but it also gives you an incentive to ignore those projects that you could stay late to work on, but which could easily wait until the next day. Relaxation is crucial for productivity – without it, we quickly burn out and have trouble getting anything done.

Depending on how you commute to work, you can maximize your productivity by using the time wisely. If you drive, you're limited to brainstorming, but great ideas often come from those moments of aimless thought. If you ride a bus, subway or train, you have more options – you can reply to emails, read reports and complete a variety of other low-priority tasks.

Sleep Hygiene

Don't fall prey to the mistaken belief that the most productive people don't sleep very much. Our society has connected sleep deprivation with dedicated workers, but in reality, even a few hours of lost sleep can have significant cognitive effects. Pozen recommends getting a full eight hours each night, even if you truly believe that your body only needs five. Numerous studies have shown that even people who are convinced that they only need a few hours of sleep actually perform at a lower level than those who get eight hours of shut-eye.

Exercise Regularly

Exercise is great for your body, but it boosts your productivity as well. Studies have shown that regular exercisers reported feeling more clear-headed than those who did not exercise. Regardless of the type of exercise you prefer (choose something you enjoy to encourage regular sessions), schedule it into your day as rigorously as you schedule your work tasks.

Productive and Efficient Business Travel

If you're like most professionals, your job will, from time to time, take you away from home. Pozen suggests that traveling within your own country can typically be handled fairly easily regarding online flight and hotel booking. International travel, however, requires some additional work in order to ensure everything goes as planned. In either case, if you have an assistant, delegate most of these details to your assistant. Major things to consider are your passport and visa, bringing adequate business cards, and even mundane details such as electrical adapters.

International travel benefits greatly from a professional travel agent. Those online flights are great deals, but can often be found through an agent just as easily. Agents are more likely to know the ins and outs of actually getting around in your destination country. Small details can make or break a business trip, and learning about them through a travel agent is a small price to pay.

Pozen also advocates having or finding a contact in the country you'll be visiting. Cultural differences are vast and what seems friendly to us may be highly offensive to a foreign business contact. In addition, many business structures that we're familiar with are operated very differently in other countries. Ideally, your contact should be somebody who works for a branch of your company and is based in your destination country. If you can't find anybody, research local customs as best you can via books and the internet.

At the Airport

Pozen recommends avoiding checking luggage at all costs. In most cases, everything you need for a business trip can fit into carry-on luggage. The bag you keep with you on the plane is also important; a flexible bag holds more and is lighter than a traditional suitcase. Pack some on-board essentials like a sleep mask and earplugs to make sleeping easier. Take advantage of any downtime by packing reading material, your laptop or anything that makes working during these periods of downtime easier.

Sign up for all the airline rewards you have access to in order to take advantage of the calmer lounges and shorter lines they offer. If possible, have your boarding pass printed ahead of time or downloaded to your smartphone. If you have a metal implant in your body, call ahead to see if the airport has full-body scanner options instead of traditional metal detectors. They may save you time and avoid that awkward pat-down.

On the Plane

Sleeping or working on the plane ride helps you make the most out of a limited situation. If you plan to sleep, fly business class if possible. There is less distracting activity and, more importantly, the seats are larger and recline further, letting you get deeper and more restorative sleep. Be sure to pack an eye mask and earplugs to block out distractions. Drink plenty of water to fight the effects of dry cabin air (buy your own at the airport), and avoid the dehydrating effects of alcohol and caffeine.

Productivity Away from Home

Sticking with your regular routine as much as possible is key when traveling. Plan your day the night before. Pozen suggests avoiding the party scene which has become a common part of after-hours business meetings in many countries; all that partying will only leave you tired. If you feel the drain of jet-lag, take a dip in your hotel's pool, hit the gym or drink coffee – the point is to avoid falling asleep.

Keeping Family Time Sacred

When a parent or spouse is on the road, those left at home can feel stressed. You can ease this in a number of ways. Pozen suggests returning home on a Friday to give yourself plenty of stress-free family time before returning to work. Take full advantage of phone calls and video chats and include children in travel planning so they have a more concrete idea as to where you're going and why.

Productive Meetings

A good meeting can accomplish many things. Unfortunately, many of the meetings we hold and attend are time-consuming, accomplish little and ultimately waste resources. Before you call or agree to attend to a meeting, make absolutely sure that your objectives can't be handled through a phone call or via e-mail. If you don't have a clear idea of why you're calling a meeting, don't call it.

If you're an employee without the freedom to pick and choose which meetings to attend, try to subtly multitask by checking e-mails or doing some other low-level activity during meeting lulls.

Video chats, often called video conferences, are a huge time-saver. Take advantage of this technology whenever possible. Pozen suggests that the only two instances that truly require in-person meetings are establishing a brand-new personal relationship and debating an issue.

Don't be afraid to decline requests for meetings; just do it with some tact. Even meetings scheduled by your boss are negotiable if you have a good working relationship. Of the meetings you do call or attend, make an attempt to keep them under ninety minutes. Past this point, attendees become bored and very little gets accomplished.

Pozen outlines five simple steps to ensure necessary meetings run smoothly:

Have a clear agenda of desired outcomes.

Begin the meeting with a brief (10 to 15 minute) overview of the meeting's goals.

Allow every attendee to debate the issues at hand – if they aren't important enough in the company to have a say, why are they attending? Likewise, senior attendees should not dominate the conversation.

Avoid jargon or muddled speech. Everybody should speak their mind clearly so that there is no question where a person stands.

At the end of the meeting, the person in charge should recap what was discussed, what was decided and what will be done. Assignments, if there are any, should follow.

When planned and executed properly, a meeting can get a lot done in a relatively short amount of time. However, if there is no real reason to call one, spend your time doing something truly productive.

Key Points of Extreme Productivity Section 2

When scheduling, use a calendar, make plenty of notes and give yourself free time.

Create a routine for simple everyday tasks.

Prepare as much as you can the night before.

Exercise regularly for increased brain power.

Get a full 8 hours of sleep each night, sleep extra hours if you experience insomnia and take a nap during the day for a boost.

Protect your family time.

When traveling, make a to-do list that can be reused for each trip, including mundane details such as what to pack. Delegate as many of these as possible.

Learn vital information about your destination.

Plan ahead for a driver to meet you at the airport and be aware of the local traffic conditions.

Have a clear goal for each trip and ensure your schedule furthers that goal.

Never check luggage, and include sleep aids, work materials and reading materials in your carry-on bag.

Fly only business class for overnight flights and stay fully hydrated.

Exercise, swim or drink coffee to fight jet lag.

Stick to your routine even when traveling.

Stay in close contact with your family to minimize the stress of frequent travel.

Politely turn down meeting invitations if they serve no real purpose and share information via the phone or email instead.

Keep meetings under ninety minutes and give people time to read any necessary materials well before the meeting itself.

Stick with Pozen's five key points of successful meetings to ensure that yours run smoothly, produce results and don't waste time.

Extreme Productivity Section 3

Personal Skills For Productivity

Reading, writing and speaking are three personal skills that no professional can afford to be without. While they seem rather basic at first glance, there are efficient and inefficient ways to perform these tasks. This section focuses on sharpening these skills in their professional and work-related aspects.

Reading for Success

Pozen asserts that realizing the purpose behind your reading is key to reading efficiently. If you know what you're looking for, you can quickly identify it, focus on it and skip the rest.

There are several main reasons for work-related reading. These include:

Understanding new ideas – things that may relate to your job in the future. These are best skimmed to gain a base knowledge.

Finding specific facts – in preparation for a meeting, for example, you may need to closely read relevant reports and memos.

Finding new information sources – links and references within articles can lead you to new sources of information that you can later review.

Unique professional reading – depending on your job, this last category can vary a great deal. Make sure you know exactly why you're reading something (checking for errors, preventing misinformation) before you begin.

There are three main steps to effective reading. First, read the introduction and conclusion paragraphs. Finish by skimming the tops of each paragraph for key ideas.

Effective reading allows you to focus on the important information while briefly skimming the rest.

How is the article or book structured? Are there chapters, bold headlines or paragraph headings? These typically give you an excellent overview of the piece's main ideas and, in some cases, the bulk of the entire piece.

Reading the first and last paragraphs, once you've understood the structure, helps you to grasp the author's main ideas. Once you know where the author is headed with his or her writing, then move on to the body of the piece.

Skimming paragraph beginnings comes next. Note that this is not passive skimming, in which we move our eyes over the words but don't really absorb anything. Productive skimming is a very active task. At each paragraph, ask yourself whether the first sentence leads you to believe that this paragraph will help further your understanding of the topic. If not, skip it and move to the next.

Remembering What You Read

During and after your reading, ask yourself what you need to remember. Write down these facts or ideas to keep yourself on track as you read. In reading lengthy or complicated pieces, your list might be quite long and involve several steps; this is fine, as long as everything is relevant and you come away with the understanding and knowledge you need.

Productive Writing

Writing is a key skill that, unfortunately, many professionals are lacking. Poor writing skills can make you look unprofessional, frustrate your customers and co-workers and create a lot of time-consuming misunderstandings due to poor communication. With emails taking the place of many phone calls, good writing skills are more important today than ever before.

Outlines

Creating an outline for anything, be it a speech or an article, is an essential part of productive writing. First, brainstorm some ideas and write them down, without worrying about order. Next, organize those ideas into groups. Creating your outline – the final step – consists of putting these groups into an order that most clearly communicates what you're trying to say.

Structuring

A well-structured article is easy and enjoyable to read. A confused one is frustrating and a big drain on your readers' time. Thankfully, structuring your piece properly is very simple. Obviously, your introduction comes first. Pozen suggests that a good introduction does three things – delivers proper context, plainly explains the author's main ideas and explains how the piece is structured.

Summaries and Conclusions

These terms are often used interchangeably when they're actually quite different things. A summary is a condensed version of the entire article, restating the main points. A conclusion leads the reader somewhere beyond the article by suggesting future implications, suggesting further reading or otherwise taking the reader's mind beyond what they've just read.

Summaries and conclusions are greatly helpful to the majority of people who will be reading your work, so put effort into making them concise, clear and easy to read and understand.

Body

The body of an article is everything between the introduction and conclusion. As with all steps of effective writing, the body of your article needs to support the effective reading steps you've just learned. This means using clear subtitles or headings to easily separate and define different parts of the body and giving readers a concise first sentence for each paragraph to make for easy skimming.

Sentences

Now that you know how to structure your piece, creating clear and effective sentences becomes critical. A good sentence has several aspects. It must be relatively short, concise, use accurate words, and be free of any spelling or grammatical errors.

Shorter sentences are simply easier to read. Run-on sentences, in which several shorter ideas are strung together, are confusing for the reader.

Active, precise, and accurate wording enhances clarity. Ensure that your readers know who is doing what in a sentence. Using the words "he" or "she" is fine, as long as the specified person is clear.

Poor spelling and grammar can quickly take a written piece from professional to high school. While electronic spell-checks and grammar programs can be helpful, they can also miss common errors. Sharpen your own spelling and grammar skills so that you can give all your writing a thorough check before finalizing anything.

Writing requires concentration, so try to find a quiet, peaceful time with few distractions. Remember that writing is a process, so don't expect to create a perfect final draft on your first try – be prepared to edit and revise. Break up the task into easily completed segments, and remember to keep your piece as short as possible.

Effective Speaking

Speaking is an amazingly effective professional tool. A good speaker can energize a meeting and clearly communicate his or her points. A poor speaker, however, can quickly bore their audience and lose track of the main objective of their speech. Pozen outlines several key steps for preparing and delivering an effective speech.

Audience

Who will your audience be? Why will they be attending, and what will they be looking to get out of the event? Is your talk intended to inform or entertain? Answering these questions will give you a good idea of how to structure your speech.

Structure

A speech has no headlines or subtitles; it's up to you to clearly convey your ideas. Structure is key in doing this effectively. Begin with an introduction, for which Pozen suggests four clear segments.

Your personal introduction should be short and sweet, clearly conveying who you are. This portion is often read by somebody else in more formal situations.

Your opening should warm your audience up. First, express gratitude for the speaking invitation and then include a short, personal, humorous story to break the tension common to formal speaking engagements.

Your explanation should be very clear – why should your audience care what you have to say?

Stating your outline comes next. Clearly explain the structure of your speech. If you're proposing, arguing, defending or suggesting something, state it before moving into the body of the speech itself.

Body Structure

The structure of your speech's body will vary depending on the occasion and topic. It should clearly progress from one idea to the next. Remember that virtually every speech is an appeal; identify what you want your audience to learn or believe and focus on those ideas. Use emotion when appropriate, just don't overdo things or become too theatrical. Use real-world examples instead of boring statistics whenever possible. End your speech somewhat emotionally when appropriate – this creates a more lasting effect in listeners' minds than simply restating what you've just said.

In your conclusion, drive home whatever you feel the key points of your speech are – the things you really want listeners to remember. Make your second-to-last statement something simple, emotional and concise.

Your final statement should be a brief but polite thanks to the host and attendees.

Practice

With your outline created, it's time to practice. Resist the urge to write every word down – this creates a boring speech and a bored audience. Stick to your outline, which gives you more room to improvise while providing a solid basis to follow.

You might feel a bit silly practicing your speech out

loud, but it's the only way to become comfortable in your delivery. It also gives you a chance to identify and change potential weak spots. Enlist a friend or colleague you can trust to give honest feedback or, if no practice audience is available, use a mirror.

Speech Day Preparation

On the day of your speech, Pozen suggests completing the following steps.

Review the attendee list and, if applicable, the conference agenda to make sure your speech will be well-received.

Give your speech a final read-through practice run.

Review the day's headlines for anything relevant to your speech. You may want to alter or add something based on relevance.

Choose equipment that allows you to walk around the room as you speak. This enhances energy and makes your audience feel engaged. If you stand perfectly still at the front of the room, your speech will take on the boring feeling of a college lecture.

Ensure that all your equipment – slides, microphone, handouts – are prepared and in their proper places.

Immediately before you take the stage, find a mirror for a last-minute appearance check. This is not a time to inadvertently leave your zipper open.

During Your Speech

Keeping your audience engaged is crucial. Ask them questions and feel them out as you speak. Smile and convey your energy; this will energize the audience. Walk up and down the aisles, directly addressing attendees (avoid being too intense, which can be interpreted as intimidation).

If you're going to use visuals in your speech, keep them relevant, engaging and brief. Never read your visuals to the audience – they can seem them as clearly as you can. Instead, use them as introductions to key points.

Keep your speech as short as is possible and appropriate. Likewise, never go over your pre-determined time – this is a quick way to irritate and annoy your audience and your host.

Questions and Answers

Plan plenty of time for a Q&A session after your speech, if appropriate. Pozen suggests the following guidelines for a productive Q&A:

Ensure that every question is heard by every attendee. If somebody speaks very softly, repeat the question so the whole room can hear.

Avoid letting a single person run the show – you may want to "plant" some questioners in the audience to call on if this becomes an issue.

Stuck for an answer? Repeat the question – this gives you time to think and makes your answer appear more thoughtful.

Don't babble – the person asking the question may appreciate a mini-speech in response, but the rest of the audience may be uninterested.

Don't let things get stale. When you see only a few hands up, announce that it's time for one last question, answer it and move on. A room full of people with nothing to ask is rather awkward. Wrap things up with an energetic sentence or two and be done.

Remember that public speaking is one of the most common fears in the world. The only way to improve is through practice, so take each snag and misstep as a learning experience.

Key Points of Extreme Productivity Section 3

When Reading -

Realize why you're reading something and what you want to gain before you begin. Concentrate on those points.

Forget traditional "speed reading" and increase your efficiency by focusing on fewer, but more important, words and sentences.

Pay attention to structure, introductions and conclusions before the body of the article. In the body, skim paragraph headlines to determine whether they're worth reading.

Focus on and write down what you want to learn or remember.

When Writing -

Create an outline – brainstorm, categorize, then organize.

Include context, theme and organizational style in your introduction.

For lengthy pieces, create a short but thorough summary.

Write for effective reading – create comprehensive first sentences for each paragraph.

Conclude by summarizing and by taking your reader's mind beyond the article.

Keep sentences short, clear and concise. Grammar and spelling should be perfect.

Accept the need for revisions.

Keep articles only as long as they need to be, and break up lengthy pieces into easy segments to avoid frustration.

When Speaking -

Use humor to engage your audience.

Introduce your speech using relevance and conclude it with emotion and key points.

Practice until you're comfortable, but avoid writing down your entire speech.

Arrive ahead of time to get a feel for your audience, calm you nerves and make last-minute preparations.

Keep your audience engaged by mingling, keeping it short and allowing time for a lively Q&A session.

Extreme Productivity Section 4

Productive Professional Relationships

Creating positive, productive, and healthy relationships with your co-workers and bosses is key to a successful career. This section helps manage your work relationships, whether you're a CEO or an entry-level employee.

Effective Managing

For top managers and anybody with a team beneath them, good working relationships are key to accomplishing goals. Pozen asserts that one of the biggest stumbling blocks in employee relations is a lack of progress recognition. Most companies recognize successes and failures, but studies have shown that employees feel the most motivated when they are making progress, even in very small ways.

Supporting your employees' progress is crucial.

Delegation is part of progress. It allows your employees to actually accomplish something while at work, and at the same time frees up your own time for more important tasks.

Allowing employees room to think and work makes them feel engaged in group progress, rather than feeling like faceless cogs in a machine. Give broad objectives, and then let your employees think up solutions on their own.

Trust Your Employees

If you don't have a high degree of trust in your employees, you won't feel comfortable delegating. This nagging concern over whether things are getting done properly is a drain on your own efficiency, since you will constantly be distracted.

Hiring is, naturally, where to begin when it comes to quality employees. Pozen strongly recommends against delegating the hiring process. Investing the time and effort in selecting quality employees will save you time, money and resources down the road.

When interviewing, ask about a potential hire's history to gain insight into their motivation. Ask for specific and relevant work history highlights instead of generalizations. Challenge them to a friendly debate, on a topic of their choosing, to critique their method and style of thinking. Keep an eye out for creativity and potential instead of relying solely on previous experience. When checking references, make the calls personally and press for honest answers. These interview steps will lead you to high-quality candidates and weed out those with the lowest potential.

Trust Goes Both Ways

It's not enough to trust your employees – they must trust you as well. Encourage trust by following guidelines of common courtesy. Be honest, polite and thoughtful – nobody wants to work for a tyrant. Keep lines of communication open so employees feel engaged, and back this up by focusing on group goals instead of your own personal glory. In addition, letting employees know that they are trusted encourages them to trust you in return. Demonstrate this trust by allowing them their own space to accomplish broad goals.

Pozen proposes five main steps for setting your team up for independent success in group objectives.

Set Up Goals – Outline what needs to be done, but give employees as much "wiggle room" as possible in creating their own methods and deadlines. Work with them, instead of barking orders, if a specific date or other detail is required.

Properly Design Metrics – These are measurable goal-points and objectives. Structuring them properly leads to success; improper structuring leads to wasted time. Having a more in-depth system of metrics will give you more accurate results.

Supply What's Needed — In most companies, team leaders and other mid-level employees simply don't have the authority to obtain resources. A large part of effective leadership is making sure that all your employees have access to everything they need. This includes obvious, tangible items such as office supplies as well as intangible aspects such as support and guidance.

Supervise Without Smothering — Many managers don't recognize their own micro-managing tendencies. Check yourself if you find that you're analyzing every aspect for minor mistakes, giving freedom only to take it back at the first misstep or picking apart any non-traditional approaches.

Tolerance — Everybody makes mistakes. While mistakes resulting from deliberate dishonesty or laziness must be dealt with (in private), honest mistakes need to be forgiven to foster trust and creativity. Likewise, when something goes well, make sure the praise is relevant and public.

Effective Relationships with Your Boss

Creating effective relationships with your superiors

does not, as commonly thought, include becoming a lap dog. These relationships will never be equal since your superiors are, by definition, superior to you in the professional world. They can, however, be mutually beneficial. Your boss can be a resource if "managed" correctly.

Proper Communication

Knowing exactly what is expected of you is critical to being an effective employee. Pozen recommends making a ranked list of your objectives, giving it to your boss for review and ensuring that your goals and priorities match up.

Reviewing this list weekly will ensure that you don't waste time working on something your boss has deemed less important. In addition, ask for critical feedback. Many bosses hesitate to critique employees out of a desire to avoid conflict. Ask for critiques regularly and, if your boss tries to brush you off with generalizations, politely ask him or her to get specific.

Type of Communication

Is your boss a fan of in-person meetings? Do they favor e-mails over phone calls? Prefer a hard copy over an electronic document? Whatever your boss's communication preferences are, be sure to accommodate them and re-check daily to see if anything has changed. Syncing your communication style boosts productivity in two ways. You won't be inadvertently irritating your boss with a communication style he or she hates, and you're more likely to get a timely response.

Supervisor Relationship Basics

The simplest way to make your boss happy is also the most obvious – consistently turn in high-quality work. This single objective will lead to raises, praise, and promotion in most circumstances.

Working well with others is also a huge factor in employee-supervisor relations. A fiercely independent worker in a team-oriented company is difficult to supervise. Likewise, if you're asked to do mundane tasks such as fetching coffee, do it. Unless you're being unfairly singled out for these types of tasks, refusing them will make you look like a diva who is "above" her co-workers.

When things go wrong, staying in a favorable light is still entirely possible. Warn your boss, if possible, when a project seems to be circling the drain. Take full responsibility for anything you've done or anything done under your own supervision – nothing screams "bad employee" like avoiding responsibility.

There is a fine line between becoming a lap dog and giving your supervisor genuine praise. Learn the difference and praise or support your boss whenever it's appropriate – just as you'd like them to do for you.

Disagreeing Without Conflict

Every now and then you will disagree with your supervisor; there's no way around the occasional difference of opinion. How you handle these differences is what matters. Planning and communication can help avoid the vast majority of disagreements. Just let your boss know what your plans are. This gives them time to object or voice their opinion before you proceed.

When genuine conflicts do come up, tackle them with diplomacy. Avoid raised voices, blame or any provoking tactics and keep things friendly. Tackling issues this way helps to ensure that even if your boss does "win" a particular battle, you won't lose your job in the process.

Bad Bosses

We live in an imperfect world, which means that you may have to answer to somebody severely lacking in good managerial skills. Pozen suggests tactics for dealing with the most common types of bad bosses.

Micro-Managing – If your boss is impossibly picky, double-check your own performance to make sure there's not a legitimate reason. If your work is up to standard, or if your boss behaves this way with the entire office, it's most likely not a personal affront.

Take the bull by the horns and ask for a private meeting with your boss to discuss these tendencies. Many micro-managers are not aware of their actions and will respond surprisingly well to such a discussion.

Neglectful – Some bosses go to the other extreme and virtually ignore their employees, leaving them guessing at what is expected. In this case, stand up for yourself and directly ask for more guidance. If you receive a project with vague goals and no structure, for example, specifically ask how he or she wants things done.

Abusive – Angry, screaming, stomping bosses are the hardest to deal with. If you have one, developing some "survival skills" is crucial. The most important thing to remember is that unless you are directly provoking your boss through your own abuse, their temper tantrums have nothing to do with you. You can also observe what provokes a blow-up and avoid those situations as much as possible.

Complaining or Leaving

If things in your work environment are severely abusive, unfair or otherwise intolerable, your only remaining option is to complain to the company's human resources department. Make no mistake about it; this will anger your boss. Keep your complaint short, truthful and to the point.

If you decide to leave the company, go about it in a respectful and responsible manner. Have another job lined up if at all possible. Give at least one month's notice and be proactive during this "limbo" time — offer to help wherever possible, show your replacement how things get done, and be sure to complete any of your own projects.

Key Points of Extreme Productivity Section Four

For Bosses -

Delegate as much as possible so you can focus on goals.

Outline employee goals, but give them freedom to create or modify deadlines, metrics and other specifics.

Hire high-level employees yourself to foster trust right from the beginning.

Build trust through communication, courtesy and common sense.

Without taking back control, monitor projects as they progress.

Mistakes happen — tolerate honest ones. Reserve criticism and punishment for deliberate dishonesty, laziness, or other clear violations. Address these concerns in private.

Give out plenty of honest praise, and do it publicly.

For Employees -

Ensure that your expectations, priorities and communication styles mirror that of your boss.

Let your boss know about your successes, alert them to future issues and take full responsibility.

Stay loyal, friendly and avoid going over your boss's head unless all other avenues are exhausted.

When conflicts do arise, pick your battles carefully, discuss issues privately and remain calm and collected.

For problem bosses, try to privately address the situation. Only if repeated attempts fail, consider leaving or complaining to HR. If you do leave, do so respectfully and responsibly.

Extreme Productivity Section 5

Life Productivity

This section shows you how to extend productivity beyond the office. Pozen discusses lifetime career planning and creating more personal time.

Career Options

Although it's tempting to plot out your entire career, Pozen cautions that this rarely, if ever, actually works out as planned. Due to fluctuations in the job market, the economy and our own preferences, the vast majority of professionals end up in a position that they never expected.

With smart and flexible career planning, this position can be a great one. If your plans are too rigid, however, you may be setting yourself up for frustration and disappointment.

Approach career planning as success planning. Planning for success is very different than choosing a single career and focusing on it when there may be different and better opportunities on your professional horizon. Pozen also points out that smart career planning is an ongoing process, changing along with the job market and other factors.

How to Begin

There's nothing wrong with having some goal career points or jobs, as long as you arrive at them after some critical thought. To formulate your list, focus on three aspects: interests, skills and the job market.

Interpreting your interests can be simplified by thinking about specific factors. What do you enjoy? Are you better with words or numbers? Are you goal-oriented or detail-oriented? A team player or a loner? Do you prefer a schedule or freedom in working hours? What are your values?

Answering these questions should leave you with a long list of possibilities. If you are young or in the middle of a mid-life career change, your list should be very broad. Those in established jobs that they enjoy will have smaller lists, but they should still include plenty of options within your company and chosen career field.

After your list is compiled, learn as much as possible about each of your potential options. Use the internet, visit job fairs, speak to people who already have the job you're interested in and, if possible, visit a career counselor. As you gather information, you'll narrow your list considerably.

Assessing Your Skills

This is a time to be extremely honest but also creative. What do you have to offer? Some prerequisites are very clear – such as obtaining a Master's degree in order to teach at the collegiate level. Other skills and requirements, such as the ability to relate to a broad range of people, are extremely valuable but not measured by a certificate or degree.

Avoid the trap of setting your sights on a career that is extremely hard to break into. This is particularly common among young people. As much talent as you may have in singing or football, the chances of turning that talent into a career are slim at best due to the huge number of competitors. Don't give up on your dreams, just think about them rationally and always have a backup plan.

How easily you can obtain job skills is another consideration. Does your dream job involve years of intense study and training, or an eighteen-month certification course? Determine how much time and money you're willing (and able) to invest in gaining skills.

The Job Market

How much demand is there for your options? Some fields are virtually exploding with growth, such as sustainable energy and technology. Others are dying a slow death. It doesn't make sense to invest time, energy and money into a useless degree.

Your Next Steps

Pozen asserts that once your list is completed and researched, keeping your options maximized should be your main goal. The more you narrow your options, the less chance you have of becoming successful due to the ever-changing nature of the job market.

Education, for most, is crucial. If you have a definite goal in mind, such as becoming a doctor, then your education is fairly clear-cut. If you're not sure where you want to be in ten years, education will still serve you well. On average, each year of education brings more than eight percent overall lifetime pay increase.

Pozen recommends avoiding the urge to specialize too early in your career or education, and putting your early formal efforts into more difficult subjects. These are subjects that can't easily be learned through independent reading, such as science and math. Focusing on one of these subjects will broaden your options, since most can be applied to a wide variety of careers.

Learning While Working

Every job you hold is a step toward your goals. Even if you hate it, you've learned something! Jobs that are broader will generally serve you better than narrow, niche fields. Pozen uses the example of corporate taxation as a subject that can be valuable to a very broad range of companies in many different industries.

Career Progress

When thinking about your next job, always keep your options in mind. Will this position bring you closer to your lifetime goals? A good way to begin is to gain management experience. This doesn't necessarily mean working as a manager. Good leadership qualities are always in demand and will serve you well in a wide variety of industries. Take up every opportunity to lead, think creatively and come up with problem-solving solutions, even if these are not part of your everyday work. You'll impress your superiors and gain valuable life skills.

The World is Shrinking

Our world is shrinking with technology, bringing together countries from across the globe. In order to compete in this new type of job market, expanding your knowledge of other cultures is essential. If you have the opportunity, spend time in different countries, or at least learn about their culture, customs and traditions. An employee with a broad knowledge of global affairs is very attractive to an employer who deals internationally.

Work for Different Types of Companies

If you've only worked in a small-store retail setting, your skills are not that attractive to the hiring manager of an international retailer. Likewise, a string of jobs at non-profit organizations don't prepare you very well for a career in corporate law. While each position brings valuable skills, avoid pigeonholing yourself into a single type of organization.

Networking

This term has gotten muddled in a sea of corporate lingo, but all it really means is increasing your number of contacts. You can go about this in many ways. Take part in conferences, committees, being sure to exchange contact information with those you meet. Take time to build and nurture relationships with your co-workers and others within your own company and field. The more people you know, the more often you'll come to mind when a new job opens up.

Goal Revising at Every Stage

Remaining flexible is key, whether you're still in college or well-established in your career. For those just starting out, Pozen cautions that not every step will be a well-paying one. If a job gives you experience, contacts, or insider knowledge of your chosen field, it will pay off in the long run even if your current paycheck is quite low.

A yearly career "checkup" can help you determine if your current position is furthering your lifetime goals, even if you're well into a long-term professional career. A great deal can change in a single year of work.

Consider the following questions when performing your assessment. Have your desires or aspirations changed? Externally, what affected your job or field? What can you learn from this? How do these external and internal changes affect your lifetime goals? As a result, how will the next year be different? Are you gaining useful skills, knowledge or experience? Do you enjoy your current field? Where do you want to be in a year? Five years? Ten?

Your answers will give you a clearer picture of whether advancing in your current field or making a switch will better serve your lifetime goals.

Retirement

As the economy changes and our life expectancy increases, more people than ever are working well into their seventies. This trend requires a different type of planning. While the financial side is fairly clear, many people want to continue working simply for something to do. Relaxing in a Florida retirement community is not their idea of a satisfying life.

During your last ten years of "official" work, your goals should include finding something that will keep you mentally alert, stimulated and satisfied after you retire from full-time employment. This may be a part-time position in your current company, an entirely new field that has always interested you, or dedicating yourself to charity organizations. Less formal approaches are also viable, such as turning a beloved hobby into a retirement career. Give yourself plenty of time to make this decision.

External Changes

External forces can make a huge impact. Recessions, foreign economies, demographic shifts, and a host of other factors can affect any employee at any company.

It's not enough to plan to survive change. To maximize your lifetime productivity and options, you must be prepared to capitalize on changes and use them to your advantage.

This may include making a career change, a shift within your company, or gaining new skills. You can capitalize on external changes in many ways. Within your company, actively look for ways to keep on top of trends and changes. For example, if no one has yet seized the opportunity to advertise via social media, be the first one to suggest it and you may find yourself heading up a new department.

What Should Remain

In our ever-changing economic world, there are two factors that should not change – your understanding of financial fundamentals and your personal integrity. The need for profits never changes – don't be blinded by fancy plans that sound great on the surface but don't offer a solid base.

Your personal integrity should also remain steadfast and unchanging throughout your career. A good reputation as an honest, diligent and reliable worker hugely benefits your future options. Reputations are also very easily ruined, so resist the urge to take that single dishonest step – the results could be devastating.

Home and Work – The Big Picture

What is the ultimate point of all this productivity and planning? For most people it's the ability to spend less time at work (while still producing quality results) and more time at leisure, with friends, family or whatever is most important to you.

Determining Your Values

To determine what you place the most value on, take a few minutes to write down how much time you spend each week on activities related to work, family, community and yourself. Next, Pozen suggests imagining that you have five spare hours. How would you spend those hours? Your answer is a fairly accurate picture of what you value most.

If you're like most, you'd prefer to spend more time with loved ones and friends. This means finding or creating a more flexible work environment. If at all possible, choose a job with a company that allows flexibility in scheduling, including specifics like caring for a sick child and maternity/paternity leave.

Protecting Family Time

Work within the confines of your job to carve out more family time. Pozen suggests making it a rule to always get home in time for dinner.

Given all the studies and statistics on how constant long hours and travel can affect family life, learn to stand up for your personal time as assertively as you would for any work-related issue. Learn to say no without creating conflict and you may be surprised at your superiors' reactions.

Caring for Home and Kids

Any professional with children knows that there simply is not enough time to devote yourself fully to work and to your children. Therefore, a reliable source of childcare or a spouse who primarily cares for the children is a must. There's no need for a full-time stay-at-home spouse; many "caretakers" have part-time careers. One way or another, however, one partner should be primarily dedicated to caring for children.

Pozen suggests networking with other parents in your office and your children's' schools. These contacts can offer coverage for emergencies, resources for baby-sitters, and many other last-minute life-savers.

Setting Boundaries in Your Mind

With all our electronic devices, it's easier than ever to never truly stop working, even while spending time with family and friends. Be decisive and clear with yourself regarding your work and personal lives. If this means placing your smartphone in a different room during dinner, do it. Whatever steps you need to take in order to achieve balance are well worth the effort.

If you must do some work at home, create very clear boundaries around it and stick with them unless there's an emergency. Sometimes, just setting up these boundaries helps you to realize what is and what is not essential. In today's world, where everything seems to be a top priority, this clarity can be a real eye-opener and a big help in separating your work from your personal life.

Key Points of Extreme Productivity Section 5

Career Planning -

Avoid being too rigid. Accept that your career will most likely be a series of changes.

Be honest in evaluating your skills, desires and talents in relation to the job market.

Research a prospective career very carefully before committing.

Keep your options open by choosing a job with broadly applicable skills.

Choose jobs with leadership, travel or different organizational structures to further expand your marketable skills.

Accept that less-than-ideal jobs are often necessary in furthering your lifetime goals.

Routinely revise your career goals, incorporating any changes, to keep yourself on track. This includes thorough planning for retirement.

Always be on the lookout for new opportunities for your company — you may end up heading a new project or department.

Remember that financial basics and your personal integrity do not and should not change.

Striking a Balance -

Create a set time to leave work each day, ideally in time for dinner at home. Guard this family time assertively.

Emergencies will occur — ensure your boss trusts that you will get all your work done if you have to take a few hours or days off.

Support for child-raising is essential. You'll need either a supportive spouse or external childcare. A supportive network at work and school is also extremely helpful.

In instances where you must work from home, establish clear boundaries and stick with them to keep your work and personal lives separate.

Shortcut Summaries strongly encourages you to buy and read the full version of Extreme Productivity by Robert C. Pozen for much more information on this topic. You'll also get all his interesting personal stories and much more detail on this topic to help you become extremely productive.

Other Productivity Books by Shortcut Summaries

If you enjoyed Extreme Productivity, be sure to get the Bestselling summary of David Allen's Getting Things Done:

Getting Things Done: A Summary of David Allen's Book on Productivity by Shortcut Summaries

Recommended Reading List

Books on Time Management

168 Hours: You Have More Time Than You Think by Laura Vanderkam

18 Minutes: Find Your Focus, Master Distraction, and Get the Right Things Done by Peter Bergman

Creating Time: Using Creativity to Reinvent the Clock and Reclaim Your Life by Marney K. Makridakis

Eat That Frog! by Brian Tracy

First Things First by Stephen R. Covey

If I'm So Smart, Why Can't I Get Rid of this Clutter? by Sallie Felton

Margin: Restoring Emotional, Physical, Financial, and

Time Reserves to Overloaded Lives by Richard A. Swenson MD

Procrastination by Jane B. Burka

Ready for Anything: 52 Productivity Principles for Getting Things Done by David Allen

Tell Your Time: How to Manage Your Schedule So You Can Live Free by Amy Lynn Andrews

The 7 Habits of Highly Effective People by Stephen R. Covey

The Dip: A Little Book That Teaches You When to Quit (and When to Stick) by Seth Godin

The Now Habit: A Strategic Program for Overcoming Procrastination and Enjoying Guilt-Free Play by Neil Fiore

The One Minute Manager by Kenneth H. Blanchard, Spencer Johnson

The Skinny on Time Management: How to Maximize Your 24-Hour Gift by Jim Randel

Time Management from the Inside Out by Julie Morgenstern

Time Management: How to Get More Done in Less Time by Craig Ballantyne

Time Management Tips: 101 Best Ways to Manage

Your Time by Lucas McCain

Time Warrior: How to defeat procrastination, people-pleasing, self-doubt, over-commitment, broken promises and chaos by Steve Chandler

What the Most Successful People Do Before Breakfast by Laura Vanderkam

What To Do When There's Too Much To Do by Laura Stack

Productivity Books - Productivity Management

Awaken the Giant Within by Anthony Robbins

Bit Literacy by Mark Hurst

Blink: The Power of Thinking Without Thinking by Malcolm Gladwell

Execution: The Discipline of Getting Things Done by Larry Bossidy, Ram Charan

Extreme Productivity: Boost Your Results, Reduce Your Hours by Robert Pozen

Getting Things Done: The Art of Stress-Free Productivity by David Allen

Getting Organized: Improving Focus, Organization and Productivity by Chris Crouch

Goal Setting: 13 Secrets of World Class Achievers by

Vic Johnson How We Decide by Jonah Lehrer

How: Why How We Do Anything Means Everything by Dov Seidman

Organize Now!: A Week-by-Week Guide to Simplify Your Space and Your Life by Jennifer Ford Berry

Out of Our Minds: Learning to be Creative by Ken Robinson Poke the Box by Seth Godin

Switch: How to Change Things When Change Is Hard by Chip Heath

The $100 Startup: Reinvent the Way You Make a Living, Do What You Love, and Create a New Future by Chris Guillebeau

The 4-Hour Workweek: Escape 9-5, Live Anywhere, and Join the New Rich by Timothy Ferriss

The Advantage: Why Organizational Health Trumps Everything Else In Business by Patrick Lencioni

The Checklist Manifesto: How to Get Things Right by Atul Gawande

The Goal: A Process of Ongoing Improvement by Eliyahu M. Goldratt

The Oz Principle: Getting Results Through Individual and Organizational Accountability by Craig Hickman

The Power of Habit: Why We Do What We Do in

Life and Business by Charles Duhigg
Thinking, Fast and Slow by Daniel Kahneman

Zapp! The Lightning of Empowerment: How to Improve Productivity, Quality, and Employee Satisfaction by William Byham

Success Principles

Achieve Anything In Just One Year: Be Inspired Daily to Live Your Dreams and Accomplish Your Goals by Jason Harvey

Don't Sweat the Small Stuff--and it's all small stuff by Richard Carlson

Drive: The Surprising Truth About What Motivates Us by Daniel H. Pink

Imagine: How Creativity Works by Jonah Lehrer

Mindset: The New Psychology of Success by Carol Dweck

Steal Like an Artist: 10 Things Nobody Told You About Being Creative by Austin Kleon

Succeed: How We Can Reach Our Goals by Heidi Grant Halvorson Ph.D.

The Fire Starter Sessions: A Soulful + Practical Guide to Creating Success on Your Own Terms by Danielle LaPorte

The Magic of Thinking Big by David J. Schwartz
The Tools: Transform Your Problems into Courage, Confidence, and Creativity by Phil Stutz, Barry Michels

Write It Down Make It Happen by Henriette Anne Klauser

21375038R00041

Made in the USA
Lexington, KY
09 March 2013